Introducing Times and Seasons

2: The Easter Cycle

Phillip Tovey (editor)
Director of Reader Training, Diocese of Oxford,
Lecturer in Liturgy, Ripon College, Cuddesdon

Patrick Angier
Vicar of Prestbury

Andrew Atherstone
Research Fellow, Latimer Trust
Assistant Curate, Eynsham and Cassington

Colin Buchanan
Former Bishop of Woolwich

GROVE BOOKS LIMITED
RIDLEY HALL RD CAMBRIDGE CB3 9HU

Contents

Acknowledgments

We wish to thank Trevor Lloyd for his comments on our work at various stages of drafting.

The Cover Illustration is by Peter Ashton

First Impression February 2007
ISSN 0144-1728
ISBN 978 1 85174 648 4

Introduction 1

This is the second booklet in this series on the Times and Seasons provision of Common Worship.

While the first booklet looked at Christmas, this one looks at the Easter Cycle—Ash Wednesday to Pentecost (pp 209–502). This period contains the remembrance of central events in the Christian faith—the death and resurrection of Jesus and the coming of the Holy Spirit in these last days. Christians have celebrated these events in many and various ways. The Book of Common Prayer eliminated the medieval ceremonial and instead emphasized the reading of Scripture for the feasts. The Oxford Movement introduced to the Church of England much of the ceremonial of either the medieval period or the then contemporary Roman Catholic practice. It was not until 1984 that material for this period was commended by the House of Bishops in *Lent Holy Week Easter.* This proved popular and is now built upon and developed in *Times and Seasons.* As commended material, the book is more of a resource than a service book and will need local adaptation.

> *Much of the material in this book can be used in a Service of the Word*

Indeed, while looking mainly like provision for Communion liturgies, much of the material in this book can be used in a Service of the Word. Imaginative and flexible use of the material is much to be commended.

The introduction to the previous book *Introducing Times and Seasons: the Christmas Cycle All Saints' Day to Candlemas* included a discussion of missio endings, short sentences of Scripture and kinds of resources. These are important issues but will not be repeated here. If you want to know more about these areas, then please look at the previous booklet. What is perhaps more important is to look at the approaches to liturgical time that occur in this period and our acts of worship. A number of approaches have developed from different traditions:

- *A teaching aid.* Holy Week and Easter are an opportunity to teach the central doctrines of the Christian faith. The readings and services are there to proclaim the gospel.

- *A re-enactment.* The services re-enact the life and death of Jesus and so the worshippers are drawn into the meaning of the original actions. Processions with donkeys can be much like this.

- *A sacramental mystery.* The mystery of Christ living in the church is manifest in the services as the remembrance of the events of Jesus' last week brings the paschal mystery of Christ's death and resurrection into our present. Thus the grace of Christ is offered to us, that Christ might live in us.

Parishes will vary as to whether they stress one or more of these types of approach.

Celebrating these services requires careful planning and consideration of local issues. The changing social setting may mean that some find it hard to come to Good Friday services in the day and an evening service may be needed as part of the programme. However, to progress from joyful waving of palms to the celebration of the resurrection without any of the intervening story is to impoverish our understanding and participation in the paschal mystery. Remembrance entails doing things that are inconvenient, because in that way we encounter the work of Christ.

Lent

2

The season of Lent has long been observed by the Christian church as a period for self-examination and self-denial, repentance and rigorous preparation before Easter.

The precise origins of the season are lost in the mists of time, but in the early church it was an occasion for the catechizing of new converts before baptism and the reconciliation of 'notorious sinners' who had been excommunicated. Soon the whole Christian community was involved in the Bible study and penitence which characterized these six-and-a-half weeks (forty weekdays) from Ash Wednesday to the end of Holy Week. *Times and Seasons* draws together some valuable 'seasonal material' for the Lenten period, but its two major and distinctive contributions are 'The Liturgy of Ash Wednesday' and 'The Way of the Cross.'

The Liturgy of Ash Wednesday

Many congregations begin Lent by meeting together on Ash Wednesday, so *Times and Seasons* offers an appropriate Holy Communion liturgy (pp 221–235). There is a strong emphasis in the service upon personal self-examination (during extended silence) and corporate confession (both wide-ranging and specific). For example, one suggested form of confession includes the lines:

We confess to you Lord…
All our past unfaithfulness:
the pride, hypocrisy, and impatience of our lives
Lord have mercy.
Our self-indulgent appetites and ways,
and our exploitation of other people
Lord have mercy.
Our anger at our own frustration,
and our envy of those more fortunate than ourselves
Lord have mercy.
Our intemperate love of worldly goods and comforts,
and our dishonesty in daily life and work
Lord have mercy.

Our negligence in prayer and worship,
and our failure to commend the faith that is in us
Lord have mercy.

The characteristic themes of Lent are further reiterated by a 'proper preface'
before communion, which declares:

For in these forty days
you lead us into the desert of repentance
that through a pilgrimage of prayer and discipline
we may grow in grace
and learn to be your people once again.
Through fasting, prayer and acts of service
you bring us back to your generous heart.
Through study of your holy word
you open our eyes to your presence in the world
and free our hands to welcome others
into the radiant splendour of your love.

Lest we misunderstand the purpose of fasting and self-denial during Lent,
there is also a helpful emphasis upon God's grace and the assurance of his
forgiveness for all who repent and put their trust in Christ. For example, the
peace is introduced with the words

Since we are justified by faith,
we have peace with God through our Lord Jesus Christ,
who has given us access to his grace.

Imposition of Ashes

The imposition of ashes forms a memorable, though optional, part of the
Liturgy of Ash Wednesday. In the Church of England the link between Ash
Wednesday and ashes was broken at the Reformation, but in recent decades
this ceremony has returned to popularity.

In the Old Testament, dust and ashes are closely linked to the curse of death
and the fragility of life, most starkly heard in God's words to Adam after sin
had entered Eden, 'dust you are and to dust you will return' (Genesis 3.19).
The Lord sometimes judged the wicked, like the cities of Tyre, Sodom and
Gomorrah, by turning them to ashes (Ezekiel 28.18, 2 Peter 2.6). Likewise, dust
and ashes are closely linked to repentance of sin, or loss and mourning—God's
people in the Old Testament often sprinkled ashes on their heads, or sat down
(even lay or rolled) in the dust. This dramatic visual expression of intense
grief went hand in hand with weeping, fasting, wearing sackcloth, tearing
one's clothes or shaving one's head. Similarly in the New Testament, Jesus

declares, 'Woe to you, Korazin! Woe to you, Bethsaida! If the miracles that were performed in you had been performed in Tyre and Sidon, they would have repented long ago in sackcloth and ashes' (Matthew 11.21). However, he also issues a stark warning against insincere public displays of repentance, particularly relevant for the imposition of ashes, 'When you fast, do not look sombre as the hypocrites do, for they disfigure their faces to show men they are fasting. I tell you the truth, they have received their reward in full' (Matthew 6.16).

The twin themes of mortality and repentance are picked up by *Times and Seasons* for the imposition of ashes. The minister introduces this outward symbol with the words:

> Dear friends in Christ,
> I invite you to receive these ashes
> as a sign of the spirit of penitence with
> which we shall keep this season of Lent.
>
> God our Father,
> you create us from the dust of the earth.
> Grant that these ashes may be for us
>   a sign of our penitence
>   and a symbol of our mortality;
> for it is by your grace alone
> that we receive eternal life
> in Jesus Christ our Saviour. Amen.

These two themes are again emphasized in the words the minister may say to each person when the ashes are imposed:

> Remember that you are dust, and to dust you shall return.
> Turn away from sin and be faithful to Christ.

Times and Seasons suggests that brief personal prayer is also offered at the time of imposition. Usually the ash is marked on the penitent's forehead in the sign of a cross, a reminder that Jesus took the punishment for our sins by his death on the cross. Although *Times and Seasons* directs that a minister should impose the ashes, a courageous congregation may choose to receive this sign from each other (akin to a congregation serving one another at Holy Communion).

The Way of the Cross

The 'Way of the Cross' (*via crucis*), sometimes called the 'Way of Sorrows' (*via dolorosa*), has for centuries been one of the most popular forms of Roman

Catholic devotion during Lent. In the early Christian centuries, pilgrims to Jerusalem attempted to retrace the footsteps of Jesus from Gabbatha (where he was condemned by Pontius Pilate) to Golgotha (where he was crucified). Although the location of these sites is lost to history, a traditional route soon developed from the Lion's Gate to the Church of the Holy Sepulchre. Pilgrims often paused to pray and meditate on the passion of Christ along the way. This act of devotion became particularly popular during the Middle Ages, and the Franciscan monks in the Holy Land erected wooden crosses or tableaux at different 'stations' to aid prayer. Christians around the world who could not make the long and dangerous journey to Jerusalem set up similar 'stations of the cross' in their churches at home. These were eventually systematized and fixed at fourteen by Pope Clement XII in 1731. They are portrayed, for example, in Mel Gibson's Hollywood blockbuster, *The Passion of the Christ* (2004).

Reformation churches abolished the 'Way of the Cross,' partly because of its close link to medieval Roman doctrine, such as indulgences (earning forgiveness by pilgrimage and prayer). They also warned against the use of images in worship. However, in recent decades the stations have become increasingly popular in non-Roman traditions. They were reintroduced to Anglicanism by the Victorian ritualists, especially the Society of the Holy Cross (SSC), and are now included in *Times and Seasons*.

In recent decades the stations have become increasingly popular in non-Roman traditions

One of the difficulties with the traditional stations is that five of them do not appear in the Bible. For example, we do not know that Jesus fell on his way to Golgotha (let alone fell three times) or that he met his mother on the way. Likewise the story of St Veronica wiping Jesus' face with a cloth, on which he left his image (the first icon), is merely legendary. Although not personally uneasy about these traditional stations, Pope John Paul II developed an alternative series, more closely linked to the Bible's account of Jesus' passion. He used them publicly for the first time on Good Friday 1991 in the Colosseum at Rome. These alternative stations are the ones chosen for *Times and Seasons* (pp 236–256), as follows:

1 Jesus in agony in the Garden of Gethsemene (Mark 14.32–36)
2 Jesus betrayed by Judas and arrested (Mark 14.43–46)
3 Jesus condemned by the Sanhedrin (Mark 14.55–64)
4 Peter denies Jesus (Mark 14.72)
5 Jesus judged by Pilate (Mark 15.14–15)
6 Jesus scourged and crowned with thorns (Mark 15.17–19)
7 Jesus carries the cross (Mark 15.20)

8   Simon of Cyrene helps Jesus to carry the cross (Mark 15.21)
9   Jesus meets the women of Jerusalem (Luke 23.27–28, 31)
10 Jesus is crucified (Mark 15.24)
11 Jesus promises the kingdom to the penitent thief (Luke 23.39–43)
12 Jesus on the cross, his mother and his friend (John 19.26–27)
13 Jesus dies on the cross (Mark 15.34–37)
14 Jesus laid in the tomb (Mark 15.46)
15 Jesus risen from the dead (Mark 16.4–8)

It will be noticed that a fifteenth station is added, on the Resurrection, because the cross and the tomb are not the end of the story. *Times and Seasons* also provides resources for 'Stations of the Resurrection' (see below, chapter 5).

For each station, *Times and Seasons* offers a short Bible reading and a related prayer. That for the first station (the Garden of Gethsemene) is typical:

> Lord Jesus, you entered the garden of fear
> and faced the agony of your impending death:
> be with those who share that agony
> and face death unwillingly this day.
> You shared our fear and knew the weakness of our humanity:
> give strength and hope to the dispirited and despairing.
> To you, Jesus, who sweated blood,
> be honour and glory with the Father and the Holy Spirit,
> now and for ever.
> Amen.

These resources might be used in a variety of settings. They need not all be included in one service, nor indeed necessarily linked to 'stations.' For example, the prayers would fit well in a typical evangelical context, such as a Good Friday reading of Mark's Gospel, chapters 14 to 16, followed by an evangelistic address or Bible exposition. Other resources, such as penitence, praise, intercession and song may be added.

If 'stations' are to be used, there are many creative ways to portray symbolically the Good Friday events. *Times and Seasons* suggests, for example, a chalice containing wine for Station 1 ('remove this cup from me'), a pair of handcuffs for Station 2 (betrayal and arrest), and so forth. There are also countless themes running through the passion narratives, including loyalty, judgment, innocence, temptation, substitution, power, justice, mercy, sin-bearing, participation, wrath, peace, forgiveness, fear, rejection, death, isolation and victory. These are more difficult, perhaps, to portray visually, but provide vital subjects for meditation and prayer. *Times and Seasons* also recommends that the congregation move from station to station, rather than remaining seated—this can provide a greater degree of engagement and flexibility, although many churches will be restricted by the design of their buildings and will need to think 'outside the box.'

Stabat Mater Dolorosa

Times and Seasons recommends concluding each station by singing a verse of the medieval hymn, *Stabat Mater Dolorosa* ('The sorrowful mother stood'). This hymn has long been connected with the 'Way of the Cross' and meditates upon the suffering of the Virgin Mary as she watched her son die. It is a hymn of obvious emotional power, but mistakenly appeals directly to Mary for her to help us grieve at the cross, for her to guard us on the Day of Judgment, and for her to grant us the glory of paradise when we die. There are several different English versions, but leaders would be wise to choose a better hymn.

Passiontide and Holy Week

3

Introduction

The Introduction to Holy Week (p 259) is brief, and the title slightly misleading, as *Common Worship* views 'Passiontide' as running from the previous Sunday. First we need to separate out two stages in the historical development, before addressing how to keep Holy Week.

In the apostolic age, Jewish Christians probably kept the Passover just as they kept other Jewish observances. They were conscious of the original exodus and the 'exodus' (Luke 9.31) which Jesus had accomplished at the same festival. In the second century the 'quartodeciman' controversy showed that the anniversary was important. As the commemoration on the first day of the week settled down, so that particular Sunday ('Easter') became the central point of the year, and the time for baptisms. This was simply an annual remembering or highlighting of the saving events of the faith, with little or no sign of what is today dubbed 'Holy Week.'

> *Easter became the annual remembering or highlighting of the saving events of the faith*

But it was very different in the fourth century. Constantine's mother 'discovered' the true cross; later Egeria, the Spanish visitor to Jerusalem, joined in retracing the steps of Jesus. The annual commemoration was turning into a reliving of the Lord's climactic week in Jerusalem. There were appropriate responses to the successive events, leading to deep mourning on both Good Friday and Holy Saturday as a prelude to the joy of resurrection on Easter Day. In other places there could be no exact topographical retracing, but the chronological reliving of it all seems to have become irresistible.

The Anglican Reformers purged the week of most of its previously distinctive characteristics, keeping only the full-length passion narratives as the Gospel readings. The Oxford and liturgical movements set the Church of England on a fourth-century approach. *Times and Seasons* takes us further in that direction, though these texts, being 'commended' rather than 'authorized,' do not bind us absolutely to such a programme, and parishes may adapt the provisions as they see fit. In any case the 'Seasonal Material' (pp 260–267) provides a valuable quarry for many liturgical contexts.

Palm Sunday

Palm Sunday (pp 268–277) has minimal introduction. Its provision has two parts, the first celebrating Jesus' triumphal entry into Jerusalem and the second being a full Passiontide Communion liturgy.

The first part, 'The Liturgy of Palm Sunday,' is centred round the holding of palms and marching in procession with them. Traditionally the palms have been distributed before the liturgy began, mentioned in Note 2 on p 268, but the text makes no mention of 'blessing' them and mentions 'branches' rather than palm crosses. In some churches the procession (Note 1) is conducted down a street, even with a donkey, but in others as perhaps a figure of eight around the aisles. The modern tradition has been to sing *All glory, laud and honour* or *Ride on, ride on, in majesty*. Once the palm celebration is complete then the Passiontide Communion liturgy begins. The triumphal entry lies behind, and the dramatization takes us into Jerusalem, into the actual 'Holy Week.'

Monday, Tuesday and Wednesday in Holy Week

Times and Seasons make no mention of these days, but parishes which think in terms of Holy Week as a single whole do make liturgical provision. Some invite a guest preacher and leader of worship for the week, and he or she will then give shape to the liturgies, and determine the length and style of preaching to match the plan. Other parishes invite different guests for each liturgical event.

Lent, Holy Week, Easter provided forms of night prayer. They may still be used on these evenings. Useful readings would be the narrative from Luke in instalments; see the *Common Worship* lectionary 'Second service.' Parishes with a daily service of Communion will find the John 12–13 passages a very good run-in towards Maundy Thursday and Good Friday. Others may use Stations of the Cross (see chapter 2), with or without short addresses, silences, meditations, or prayers. Others again may have simply guided meditations or Passiontide addresses.

Chrism Eucharist (Maundy Thursday)

Medieval tradition has the bishop 'blessing' oils in his cathedral at a 'Chrism Mass' on Maundy Thursday, to renew the oils for Easter baptisms. After Vatican II Rome added the clergy's renewal of their ordination vows. Church of England bishops, who had sometimes had 'connoisseur' rites for Rome-inclined clergy in the 1970s, started to invite all the clergy during the 1980s. Anointing of the sick has a New Testament warrant (see also Canon B37), but oiling in baptism or confirmation has no such warrant, and little Anglican precedent. An annual diocesan rite for the oils has become overblown, for 'blessing' oil for the sick can be provided at any point (see, for example, *Pastoral Services*) and oil in initiation is simply not used in most parishes. These rites get it out of proportion, not least in the title 'chrism' which only touches the special 'confirmation' oil, but also in a further special 'slot' for 'The Reception of Holy Oils' (p 292).

Comically, the introduction (p 278) is longer than that for the rest of the Week put together. The renewal of ministerial vows, even if modern, has a clearer purpose than the oils ritual, but the *Times and Seasons* pattern is poor. The orders are addressed in this sequence: lay ministers (Form A only); deacons; presbyters; bishops. But it is arguable that the bishop as officiant should renew his commitment first, before he asks it of others. Moreover we need to ask whether taking a single question to each order in turn, and only after that asking the congregation to pray for them in turn, is a helpful pattern. Rather, let each order stand, and immediately be reminded of their call, asked to recommit, and be prayed for, before the rite goes on to the next order; this is far more satisfying.

> *It is arguable that the bishop as officiant should renew his commitment first*

The overall structure also needs re-examination. *Times and Seasons* has followed the Roman Catholic order whereby the ministerial commitment comes first and the blessing of the oils is treated as climactic. But, in an Anglican context, this is questionable, and dealing with the oils in a low-key way, before rejoicing together in God's calling to ministry, is far more satisfying. Let no diocese be mesmerized by the *Times and Seasons* order.

Maundy Thursday Liturgy

Maundy Thursday is the day of the Lord's 'Last Supper,' the name commemorating the delivery by him of his new commandment (*mandatum novum*, John 13.34, from which the word 'Maundy' is contracted). *Times and Seasons* gives a minimal introduction, but in John 13, the Gospel of the day in each year, it is the foot washing, not the institution of Communion, which dominates. So the narratives of the actual institution in Matthew, Mark and Luke do not get read then, save for the summaries within the eucharistic prayers, and thanksgiving for the institution of the Lord's Supper itself is a very secondary theme.

For the foot washing, it is helpful to ask for volunteers, perhaps from different groups, in advance and to consider the practicalities. The 'candidates' then sit on a slightly raised dais or platform, facing the congregation, perhaps in a half-moon, six to a dozen in number. Usually the clergy wash the feet of lay people. A bowl-carrier and/or towel-carrier preceding the abluting cleric may assist the process. And, despite the occasional smile, foot washing can indeed bring home God's message of the service of the strong to the needy.

The other Maundy Thursday focus has been the 'Watch.' An outline procedure is in *Times and Seasons* but, once the Communion rite is finished, the provision made is simply one of several options and parishes should freely devise their own pattern. The text attempts a formal point of having no blessing and dismissal—the time of the Watch simply goes on. Informally, of course, in many parishes people simply depart as time passes.

The rubrics and the Introduction suggest the 'stripping' of the ornaments of the Holy Table and its surrounds, and they call this space a 'sanctuary,' a term deliberately avoided in official Church of England liturgy hitherto. They suggest a procession, which might be the people passing to, say, a side-chapel chosen for the Watch. Interestingly there is no mention here of reserving sacramental elements. In most cases lights will be dimmed, perhaps even to the point of no more than a single light at the exit, and some minimal provision, by torch or candle, for reading aloud any Scripture passages.

The rite suggests two different patterns of reading; the first takes five chapters of John's gospel, and intersperses them with psalms, probably with intervals of silence. The people thus reflect on Jesus' great discourses in the upper room, and on the way to Gethsemane, but never reach the actual time in the garden and the arrest. The account of that time comes in the 'The Gospel of the Watch' which draws from the Synoptic Gospels, and may indeed follow the great discourses, but in the second pattern is read on its own with a much greater use of silence. However, any congregation is, obviously, free to arrange a Watch on whatever basis it wishes, and the use of different meditative material, even poetry or dialogue or music, is also possible.

Good Friday

Good Friday remains a public holiday in England, so main liturgical services for lay people during the day remain credible. Round the country there are several discernible patterns of observance, not all exclusive of each other, as for example:

1 The three-hour devotion from 12 till 3—perhaps centred round Jesus' 'seven words from the cross.' The tradition has been to have advertised sessions within the three hours with breaks on the hour or even on the half-hour, usually marked by hymns about the crucifixion, during which people may come and go at their discretion.

2 One-hour services, often falling within the three-hour period and echoing some part of that devotion.

3 Celebrations of Holy Communion, either within the three-hour period (as under 2 above) or at a separate time.

4 Stations of the Cross, less often reported, but obviously appropriate.

5 Ecumenical marches of witness—very often followed by services in different churches at 11 or 12.

6 Whole mornings of activity and learning on church premises for children.

7 'The Liturgy of Good Friday' as it is dubbed in *Times and Seasons*.

8 Evening services of varying character.

While this range exists, *Times and Seasons* has disregarded all but numbers 4 and 7. In *Lent Holy Week Easter* the introduction to Good Friday (on pp 196–7) said this:

> The vexed question as to whether Holy Communion should be celebrated on this day has been answered in the affirmative and provision so made… However, it is recognized that there is a strong custom and tradition in many churches that the eucharist should not be celebrated, but that Holy Communion should be given from the sacrament consecrated at the service of Maundy Thursday…

But what was a concession in 1986 has become the almost exclusive norm in 2006:

> There is not now usually a celebration of the eucharist on Good Friday; instead, consecrated bread and wine remaining from the Maundy Thursday eucharist are given in communion.

The contrast with 1986 is considerable; and, in reporting what is 'usually' done, it is highly prescriptive in that only one pattern of distributing communion follows; and it is odd in that a large proportion of the Church of England parishes would never expect to reserve consecrated bread and wine. The service refers to bread and wine, and parishes that do reserve should reserve both elements. It remains a question as to whether Maundy Thursday should be thus prolonged into Good Friday.

In the actual provision made for an ante-communion, there are three notable features, as set out overleaf.

a   The gospel reading is the Passion narrative including the whole of chapters 18 and 19 of John's gospel, previously provided in dramatic form for several voices.

b   After the sermon comes 'The Proclamation of the Cross,' a slightly softened title for the Roman 'Veneration' of the Cross. The rubrics are minimal, but hint at the bringing in of a large cross, to be planted before the people, for 'appropriate devotions' to follow. Some will address the cross physically, others will simply stand with bowed head, others again simply turn and return to their seats. Meanwhile, there is a context of responsive anthems, sung or said. The first, in two different 'versions,' is known as 'The Reproaches'; for it is cast as a deeply sorrowing Messiah puzzling and grieved over the apathy and opposition of his people. The second and third are shorter scriptural forms of adoration, and the fourth adapts Psalm 67, the Misereatur, into a context of joy in the cross. Short 'acclamations' follow.

c   The intercessions have always been a notable feature of official Good Friday liturgy, not least with an evangelistic slant.

Much of the material here is valuable, but parishes will need to draw on the materials discriminatingly and certainly not reproduce them blindly.

Holy Saturday (or Easter Eve)

Times and Seasons make no special liturgical provision for this day. The Common Worship lectionary supplies scripture readings, the theme of which is the burial of Christ. The mood of the day (terminated when an Easter Vigil begins) is that of bereavement and desolation marked by minimal liturgical engagement.

The Easter Liturgy 4

Times and Seasons gives us a variety of resources for the celebration of the Pasch: the great Easter Liturgy that leads us through the journey from the emptiness of Holy Saturday to the resurrection life of Easter Sunday (pp 321–424).

As well as familiar and less familiar liturgical resources there are detailed, informative notes and comments to guide the process of service construction and these make up nearly a quarter of the material. In addition a rich variety of rubrics within the liturgical texts complement the resource.

Times and Seasons outlines the four main elements of the Easter liturgy as we have them from the 4th century, still making a coherent whole:

- The vigil of readings and prayers—a time of waiting and preparation but also a setting out of the story of salvation;

- The service of light—proclamation of the resurrection;

- The liturgy of initiation—baptism and confirmation and the return of penitents, proclaiming forgiveness and new life in Christ;

- The liturgy reaches its climax with the first Communion of Easter. A bright joyous celebration full of light, colour and music—a visible symbol of Jesus' presence with his people.

Traditionally this was a service that began after sundown on Saturday and ran through to after dawn on Sunday. Such a long service is a challenge for modern churchgoers to attend. *Lent, Holy Week, Easter* addressed this problem by placing the vigil alone on the Saturday night whilst keeping the rest of the elements together. In some churches there was a similar separation of the renewal of baptism vows and services of baptism; others moved the whole celebration to the Saturday with the first communion of Easter falling either after midnight or sometimes just after dark.

Times and Seasons marks a return to the unified practice offering two main patterns alongside a wide variety of alternatives and choices. These resources open the door to many local creative solutions, without back-tracking on the formational benefits and possibilities of an all-night rite. There is also a helpful recognition that the Easter congregation can be one of the largest all-age congregations of the year. The introduction to *Times and Seasons* states that material taking account of children within the service has not been included in the expectation that this will be provided in the local setting. Care needs to be taken in the choice and selection of material to ensure the Easter Liturgy is not one of the longest and least accessible services for children and visitors.

Three different patterns of Easter liturgy are presented.

1 Easter Liturgy: Pattern A

This contains all four main liturgical elements but has the service of light followed by the vigil (pp 328–347).

For the service of light there is no instruction concerning the location of the fire, whether outside the building or at the east end of the church, as is many churches' tradition. There is provision for lighting the candle from a taper but there is something wonderful about gathering outside in the dark with hushed voices, the air of expectation, lighting the fire with a spark and kindling the new flame. In my experience a fire steel and tumble dryer fluff is a great way to start the Easter fire with a spark. As the fire blazes up, the president lights the candle from the flames and proclaims:

> May the light of Christ rising in glory,
> banish all darkness from our hearts and minds.

A procession into church is made behind the new Easter candle, singing the Exsultet, an Easter hymn, and then into the vigil.

The 'As we await the risen Christ let us hear the record of God's saving deeds in history…' (p 338) prayer sits a little uneasily following the proclamation of the light of Christ as the Easter candle is brought in, although using the Christological responses before the collects and positioning the reader in front of the Easter candle counters this to some extent. There is plenty of flexibility in how much Vigil material to use here, though the notes state it is 'desirable that the reading from Genesis 1 be used and the reading from Exodus 14 should always be used' (p 332). The initiation liturgy draws on the seasonal material from *Common Worship Initiation* and the Liturgy of the Eucharist from familiar sources.

2 Easter Liturgy: Pattern B

Similarly this pattern contains all four elements but the service of light follows the vigil (pp 348–371). This alleviates the anomaly of the vigil readings following the Resurrection proclamation, but if the Easter fire is to be celebrated in the dark, pushes the start time back long before dawn. Pattern B is well suited for an all-night creative approach to the vigil following one of the reading themes with full use of the wide variety of creative possibilities. Amongst the suggestions are dramatized readings, interactive Bible study and artistic activity all of which need the extra time that all night celebration would provide. The use of differing lighting schemes alongside the Bible readings and projected visual images could enhance this retelling of the story as could interactive stations and appropriate food and drink at different times through the night. This pattern enables the use of different venues and for those unable to be there for the vigil to join at the lighting of the Easter fire.

3 The Dawn Service

This provides a third option in a less worked out, flexible form appropriate for a variety of settings away from church—on a hill, riverbank, city park or place of community significance (pp 398–400). The suggestion of personal, historical and biblical stories of escape being shared is an excellent one and this use of testimony could be made use of elsewhere in the Easter Liturgies. Such services are often ecumenical and all age and so the suggestions of fireworks, party poppers, balloons, confetti and other items of celebration are well worth picking up on, as is the prayer below:

> Eternal God,
> who made this most Holy Night
> to shine with the brightness of your one true light,
> set us aflame with the fire of your love,
> and bring us to the radiance of your heavenly glory;
> through Jesus Christ our Lord.
> Amen.

For each of the options there is very useful material in the accompanying notes, with interesting and helpful suggestions and some creative thinking about where to meet. These are not exclusive to this particular service; the notes on the dawn service could equally be applied to the vigil.

The key elements of these services can now be further explained.

The Vigil

Included are five sets of readings following the themes of Baptism, Women in Salvation, Salvation, Renewal and Freedom. Each of the themes offers creative possibilities for shaping the vigil. The Women in Salvation or Baptism themes perhaps fit best if the vigil is held prior to the dawn service, as it was at that time that the women would have been preparing to visit the tomb and those awaiting Easter baptism were in their final preparations. Renewal and Baptism themes also fit well when the vigil is held on the Saturday evening and is accompanied by either baptism or renewal of baptism vows.

The importance of the vigil in telling the story is recognized in the material and it rightly highlights the need to engage with a wider cross-section of worshippers than would normally attend such services and hangs tantalizing ideas that need enfleshing. A difficult problem, with nightfall at 8 o'clock, is how to include families and single elderly people.

The prayer resources that accompany the Vigil readings have two distinct styles: the style suggested for Pattern A is a traditional collect style with a Christological emphasis familiar from *Lent Holy Week Easter*. The prayer accompanying the reading of Isaiah 55, for example, reads:

> Most Merciful God,
> who by the death and resurrection of your Son Jesus Christ delivered
>   and saved the world:
> grant that by faith in him who suffered on the cross
> we may triumph in the power of his victory;
> through Jesus Christ your Son our Lord. Amen.

In contrast, with Pattern B we are offered a style that would fit well with an informal and interactive vigil:

> Let us pray for peace and justice throughout our world:
> Blessed are you Lord God of our salvation.
> You quench the thirst of those who yearn for righteousness
> and satisfy the hunger of those who crave for justice.
> Lead your longing people back to peace,
> that with the mountains and hills
> we may burst into songs of joy,
> O Lord, our maker and redeemer. Amen.

The Service of Light

This builds upon the material in *Lent, Holy Week, Easter* with the new prayers useable in a variety of structures and a choice of prayers to use after the Easter fire is lit (p 402).

The Liturgy of Initiation

This liturgy draws on *Common Worship* Christian Initiation material. The whole text for the baptism (of those able to answer for themselves) is included as well as guidelines and suggestions for when no candidates are available.

Where baptism is included, and this has to the preferred option, no reference to confirmation or reception of communion is included.

Times and Seasons includes six further options for celebrating Easter. This is a mixed menu of assorted resources that may or may not be of use depending on particular church situations.

A Mid-Morning Eucharist on Easter Day using Elements from the Easter Liturgy

The main addition here (pp 402–403) is the incorporation of elements of the Service of Light such as the lighting of and procession with the Easter candle and the lighting of congregation members' candles. Options of either affirmation of baptismal vows or thanksgiving for the resurrection are suggested as responses after the sermon. The difficulties of presenting a service for the night during the daytime are raised but not fully resolved; perhaps an alternative could be to lay more emphasis on the baptismal elements of the Easter Liturgy as full immersion adult baptisms can be a powerful symbol of resurrection power.

An Outline Service of the Word for Easter Day

This gives outlines (pp 404–407) for both when there has and has not previously been a service of light. It offers resources to create the option of a shape that enables a response to the large numbers of potential fringe and occasional worshippers attending at Easter. A pattern for the day might commence with a first service (using either Pattern A or Pattern B) for the Easter Liturgies to begin before dawn on Easter Sunday and end with a great celebration of the first Holy Communion of Easter. This could be followed by a church breakfast, then a mid-morning Service of the Word, perhaps incorporating the prayers at the garden, geared more particularly as a seeker-style service to fringe and occasional worshippers.

Instructions for Marking the Easter Candle

The instructions are clearly outlined with a helpful diagram for both marking the *alpha/omega* and date and inserting the nails or incense studs (pp 408–409).

The Exsultet

As well as the traditional form of this Easter hymn there are responsive, metrical and other options (pp 410–417). The metrical version fits a

10.10.10.10 metre but we are advised that not all tunes of that metre are suitable and the additional text of the Franco-Roman Exsultet with its allusion to bees is curiously included.

Welcoming the Easter Candle into the Church, with Prayers at the Easter Garden

Although tucked away at the end of the section both of these resources could prove useful (pp 418–420). Where a number of churches come together at a different location to combine resources for either pattern of the Easter Liturgy, then the bringing in of the lit Easter Candle is a vitally important part of the proclamation of the Resurrection in the home church. The prayers at the Easter garden include Frank Colquhoun's lovely:

> Risen Lord Jesus,
> as Mary Magdalene met you in the garden
> on the morning of the resurrection,
> so may we meet you today and every day:
> speak to us as you spoke to her;
> reveal yourself as the living Lord:
> renew our hope and kindle our joy;
> and send us to share the good news with others. Amen.

This option gives the opportunity for both movement and action in similar ways to a crib service.

Thanksgiving for the Resurrection

This appropriately ends the section with material from *Common Worship* and the traditional Easter Anthems (pp 421–424).

One of the most familiar Easter symbols, the Easter egg, gets no mention in the material, although it is a commonly used part of many Easter Liturgies. Some churches give them to children at the communion rail during the distribution, others hand them out at the door at the close of the service and others hunt for them during the all age worship. Words to add to this common action could have been useful and similarly the practice that some American churches have of hiding the 'alleluias' over the Lenten period and then hunting for them within the Easter service could make an interesting and refreshing addition.

The Easter Season 5

Introduction

This section includes the whole Easter period from Easter Day itself to the day of Pentecost. The introduction reminds us that this is a season of joy, a festal season. It is too easy to celebrate Easter as the end of the rigours of Lent and then condense the celebration of Easter to a couple of Sundays. By half way through the Easter season it is back to ordinary worship with scarcely any celebration of the resurrection save for an odd 'alleluia.' The resources provided in *Times and Seasons* enable an ongoing celebration. Local churches will need to think about the Easter period with almost as much clarity as Lent.

The introduction also reminds us of the baptismal nature of the season. In line with baptismal ecclesiology, which sees baptism as the key event that makes us church, various actions are suggested to remind us of our baptism. Churches that have been running a nurture group in Lent will have candidates for baptism (and/or confirmation, or affirmation of baptismal faith) at Easter. *Common Worship Christian Initiation* puts this adult preparation as central to the life of the church, with the Easter baptism. Thus baptism is transformed from being an occasional office to the centre of the mission of the church. 'Rites on the Way' in *Christian Initiation* include a number of options for the incorporation of the baptismal candidates to the local congregation (pp 182–187, 193–196). *Times and Seasons* keeps a baptismal focus through the Easter candle and the symbolic use of water.

Seasonal Material

The first part of the Easter material is a resource section. This gathers material from previous volumes and includes some new texts. There are two Kyrie confessions included, but remember that *New Patterns for Worship* on page 76 includes guidance on how to write your own thematic to the day.

The absolutions include an option of sprinkling with water, with a prayer over the water, a rubric on sprinkling, and an absolution. This is to strengthen the baptismal connection appropriate for the season and the absolution as renewing the baptismal covenant.

This form of absolution may appropriately be used at the Sunday Eucharist in Eastertide.

The president prays over a vessel of water

God our Father,
your gift of water
brings life and freshness to the earth;
in baptism it is a sign
of the washing away of our sins
and the gift of life eternal.

Sanctify this water, we pray.
Renew the living spring of your life within us,
that we may be free from sin
and filled with your saving health;
through Christ our Lord. **Amen**.

The president and people are sprinkled.
Suitable hymns, songs or anthems may be sung.
The president concludes with this or another authorized absolution:

May the God of love and power
forgive you and free you from your sins,
heal and strengthen you by his Spirit
and raise you to new life in Christ our Lord. **Amen**.

This could be done in a variety of ways—people coming forward to the water and signing one another—as well as someone walking up the aisle sprinkling people. It needs an introduction to the confession that draws out the baptismal connection, particularly where people are unfamiliar with this approach.

Two extended prefaces are provided for the Eucharistic Prayer. These could also be adapted for use in Services of the Word, or as services of light with evening prayer. *New Patterns for Worship* on p 222 gives directions on how to compose your own longer thanksgiving for use in any service.

Particularly attractive and easy to miss are the three alternative dismissals. The directions are a bit sparse, but the first one could go:

He is not here. He is risen.
Go in peace to love and service the Lord. Alleluia, Alleluia.
In the name of Christ. Alleluia, Alleluia.

Stations of the Resurrection

These are called an 'emerging devotion' by the introduction, which may be a surprise to some who have never come across them before. However, the idea is easy to grasp. The use of the Stations of the Cross has become quite common both in churches and as an ecumenical devotion in Lent. The Stations of the Resurrection mirror the more well known Lenten devotion, providing an Easter devotion. Their newness will perhaps enable a flexibility of use.

Nineteen stations are given. Each station begins with an invariable response. Then there is a reading, reflection and prayer, all variable. This concludes with an invariable acclamation. These can stand alone, be a part of a Service of the Word or even be connected to a service of Holy Communion. Imaginative adaptation is required for this material, but it could be used by moving round the church visiting font, candle, Easter garden, churchyard and table. Alternatively presentations around the church could be set up as in liquid worship to form the meditations for the stations. It might be particularly useful to do this after the Easter holidays when things are back to normal to remind us that the resurrection of Christ means that things are no longer normal.

Ascension

The Liturgy of Ascension Day might at first look a bit over the top with an introduction and reading in the gathering (a bit like on Palm Sunday), alternative prayers throughout the Communion liturgy, words of fraction for the day, reading and responsory at the dismissal. If all this were done, then there certainly would be saturation with Scripture. It is of course for individual churches to select the material that they use. Some will be of help to all; few will use all.

If all this were done, then there certainly would be saturation with Scripture

This service clearly makes Ascension Day a pivotal point. It is the fortieth day of Easter, the feast of Christ's Ascension. The days afterwards look forward to Pentecost and the coming of the Holy Spirit. However, Ascension Day is not so neatly celebrated. In some places the material will need to be adapted to work with children, the church school having a service on this day, perhaps in the morning. It is a weakness of much *Common Worship* material that the dimension of children as worshippers has been rendered invisible. Also in some areas numbers attending Ascension Day evening liturgies has been declining. A new catechetical movement needs to stress the major midweek festivals as crucial. The feasts of our Lord are not optional extras or just for the keen. They say something about the very roots of our faith.

So selection of the material provided for the needs of a local church is essential. Some will want to worship with the fullness of the service, others will select a few of the options to mark the Ascension. As the focus of the coming ten days is to be preparation for Pentecost it might be particularly important to include the responsory:

As we wait in silence
Make us ready for your coming Spirit.

As we listen to your word
Make us ready for your coming Spirit.

As we worship you in majesty
Make us ready for your coming Spirit.

As we long for your refreshing
Make us ready for your coming Spirit.

As we long for your renewing
Make us ready for your coming Spirit.

As we long for your equipping
Make us ready for your coming Spirit.

As we long for your empowering
Make us ready for your coming Spirit.

The alternative dismissal also marks that change of direction:

Waiting expectantly for the promised Holy Spirit,
go in peace to love and.service the Lord. Alleluia, Alleluia.
In the name of Christ. Alleluia, Alleluia.

Seasonal Material for Pentecost

The period from Ascension Day to Pentecost looks forward to the coming of the Holy Spirit. The seasonal material provided relates to Communion liturgies, though some of it could also be used in other services. This material will be particularly of use on the Sunday after Ascension; ideally Ascension should have been left behind but in some local circumstances there might need to be an element of looking back before people can look forward. This is not going to be helped by the readings which unlike the ASB do not treat Easter 7 as a second opportunity to teach about the Ascension. Rather the focus is on the coming Holy Spirit.

The Pentecost Liturgy

The Pentecost Liturgy is again a very full provision that will need adapting to local use. *Times and Seasons* seems to have forgotten that Christian Initiation also allows the Corporate Renewal of Baptismal Vows on Pentecost (p 193). Clearly churches will have to adapt to their local circumstances. As an aside there is an interesting rubric at the end of the service, which is perhaps an example of inculturation for England: 'Weather permitting the ministers and people process out of church' (p 502).

The introduction is written in a particularly appropriate style.

> Jesus Christ, whom we worship, is our crucified, risen and ascended Lord and we have been privileged to walk with him through his journey of love.
> We have faced the agony of his suffering and death on a cross.
> We have rejoiced at his bursting free from the bonds of death.
> We have enjoyed his risen presence with us and his revelation of himself through the breaking of bread.
> We have seen his return to the throne before which every knee shall bow and every tongue confess that this Jesus is Lord.
> And now, with the followers of his own time, we wait the coming of the promised Holy Spirit, his gift to his people, through whom we make Christ known to the world.

This is not written to give information, 'Dear brothers and sisters on the day of Pentecost we...' but becomes a proclamatory text reminiscent of the festal preaching of some fathers of the church, almost turning into a thanksgiving prayer.

Prayer for personal renewal is also put in the Gathering, but some will be more used to this being available during the distribution of Holy Communion. The rubrics are a bit elusive, saying that: 'Those who wish to receive this ministry of prayer may come forward. Appropriate hymns and songs may be used' (p 493). Presumable the ministry is of the laying on of hands and anointing with oil. No particular words are given for this ministry and the directions in *Christian Initiation* 'Prayers for Individuals in Public Worship' (pp 264–265) give helpful guidance. The words that are used in both the 'anointing the sick' and at anointing in 'reconciliation and restoration' (see *Christian Initiation* p 271 and p 299) seem to miss the Pentecostal theme of the day. The text includes a blessing of oil, but if the service is not to grow to an enormous length, then using previously blessed oil would seem a sensible option.

The service ends with a thanksgiving for the light around the Paschal candle. Candles may be lit, questions of commitment may be asked and the Paschal candle extinguished, marking the end of the season.

6 Conclusions

Times and Seasons provides a rich resource for parishes in this central period of the Christian calendar.

There is new material particularly for the Easter to Pentecost period. But there are some losses from the previous *Lent, Holy Week, Easter,* not least in the provision of Lenten penitential services and the Agape with Holy Communion (see the online resources at www.grovebooks.co.uk). An adaptation of the latter, modifying it to the Service of the Word with Holy Communion, is included in the appendix.

It has to be remembered that the majority of the material is simply 'commended' and as such is not compulsory liturgy or even official Church of England doctrine. This also means that previous 'commended' material may be used (for it has not been uncommended) and that a local parish is free to adapt the services provided, as is pastorally suitable for them.

While the options provided may seem to be primarily for the service of Holy Communion, much of the material may also be used in Services of the Word. The worship leader needs to read the book with a creative eye, looking for interesting ways of adapting the texts. It is regrettable that *Times and Seasons* did not have greater interaction with *New Patterns for Worship* in its suggestions. It is hoped that this present book has gone some way to stimulating such creativity.

Bibliography

J Haselock and R Greenacre, *Using Common Worship: Times and Seasons, Volume 2* (CHP, 2007)

G Ambrose, P Craig-Wild, D Craven, *Together for a Season, Volume 2* (CHP, 2007)

P Bradshaw (ed), *A Companion to Common Worship, Volume 2* (SPCK/ Alcuin Club 2006) pp 51–107

T Lloyd, *Celebrating Lent Holy Week and Easter* (Grove Worship booklet, W 93)

M Perham and K Stevenson, *Waiting for the Risen Christ* (SPCK, 1986)

Kenneth Stevenson, *Jerusalem Revisited* (The Pastoral Press, 1988)